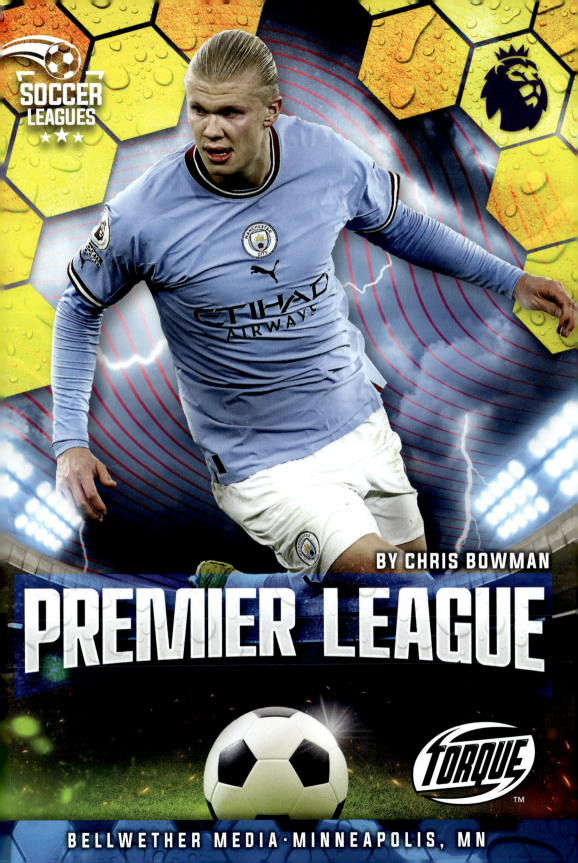

Torque brims with excitement perfect for thrill-seekers of all kinds. Discover daring survival skills, explore uncharted worlds, and marvel at mighty engines and extreme sports. In *Torque* books, anything can happen. Are you ready?

This edition first published in 2025 by Bellwether Media, Inc.

No part of this publication may be reproduced in whole or in part without written permission of the publisher. For information regarding permission, write to Bellwether Media, Inc., Attention: Permissions Department, 6012 Blue Circle Drive, Minnetonka, MN 55343.

Library of Congress Cataloging-in-Publication Data

Names: Bowman, Chris, author.
Title: Premier League / Chris Bowman.
Description: Minneapolis, MN : Bellwether Media, 2025. | Series: Soccer leagues | Includes bibliographical references and index. | Audience: Ages 7-12 | Audience: Grades 4-6 | Summary: "Engaging images accompany information about the Premier League. The combination of high-interest subject matter and light text is intended for students in grades 3 through 7"– Provided by publisher.
Identifiers: LCCN 2024022495 (print) | LCCN 2024022496 (ebook) | ISBN 9798893040265 (library binding) | ISBN 9781644879627 (ebook)
Subjects: LCSH: F.A. Premier League–History–Juvenile literature. | Soccer–History–England–History–Juvenile literature.
Classification: LCC GV943.55.F36 B69 2025 (print) | LCC GV943.55.F36 (ebook) | DDC 796.334/640942-dc23/eng/20240520
LC record available at https://lccn.loc.gov/2024022495
LC ebook record available at https://lccn.loc.gov/2024022496

Text copyright © 2025 by Bellwether Media, Inc. TORQUE and associated logos are trademarks and/or registered trademarks of Bellwether Media, Inc. Bellwether Media is a division of Chrysalis Education Group.

Editor: Kieran Downs   Designer: Gabriel Hilger

Printed in the United States of America, North Mankato, MN.

TABLE OF CONTENTS

THE TOP TWO	4
WHAT IS THE PREMIER LEAGUE?	6
HISTORY OF THE PREMIER LEAGUE	8
THE PREMIER LEAGUE TODAY	12
FAST FACTS	20
GLOSSARY	22
TO LEARN MORE	23
INDEX	24

THE TOP TWO

It is near the end of the 2022–2023 Premier League season. The top two teams, Arsenal and Manchester City, face off. City scores early on. Then they add two more **goals**.

Arsenal scores one of their own. But City scores again in **extra time**. City wins! They are one step closer to winning the Premier League title!

MANCHESTER CITY

WHAT IS THE PREMIER LEAGUE?

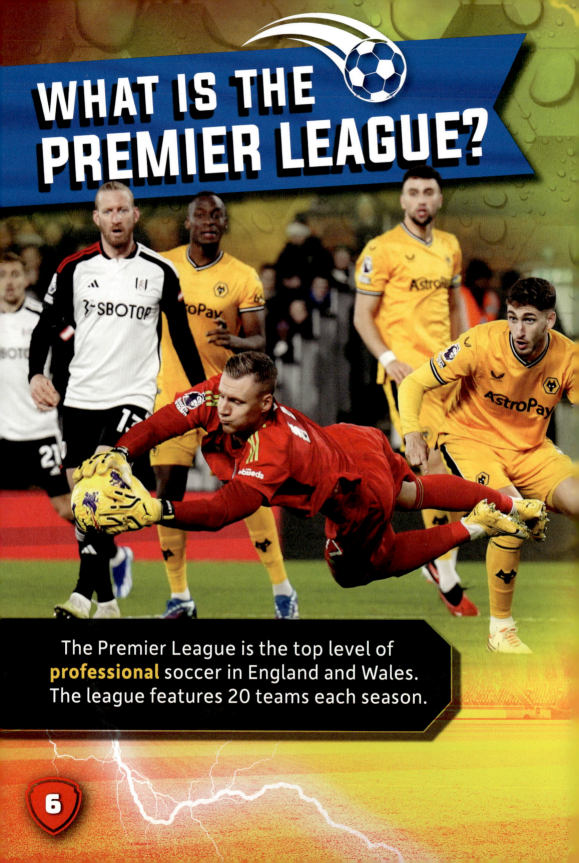

The Premier League is the top level of **professional** soccer in England and Wales. The league features 20 teams each season.

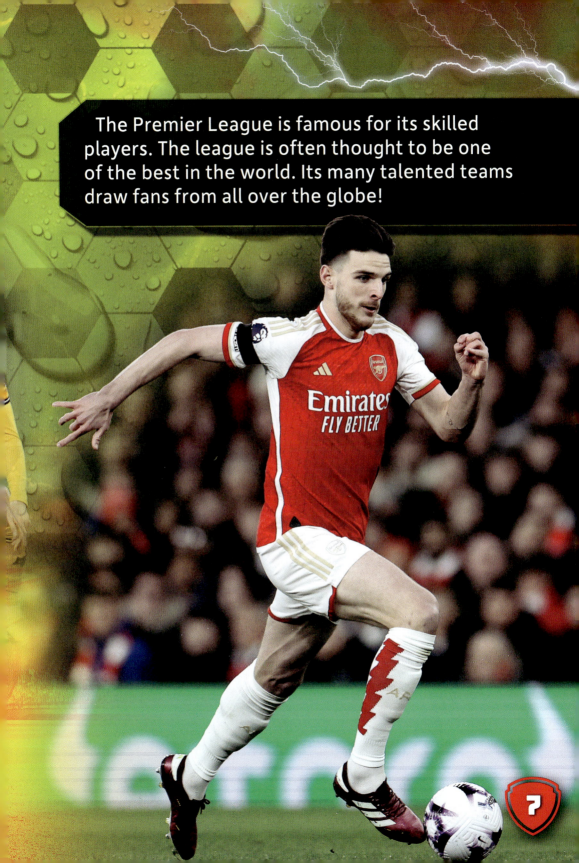

The Premier League is famous for its skilled players. The league is often thought to be one of the best in the world. Its many talented teams draw fans from all over the globe!

HISTORY OF THE PREMIER LEAGUE

The top soccer level in England and Wales was once the first **division** of the English Football League.

In 1991, the top teams agreed to start a new league. They hoped to attract better players. They also wanted to bring in more money. The teams formed the Premier League. Its first season began in 1992.

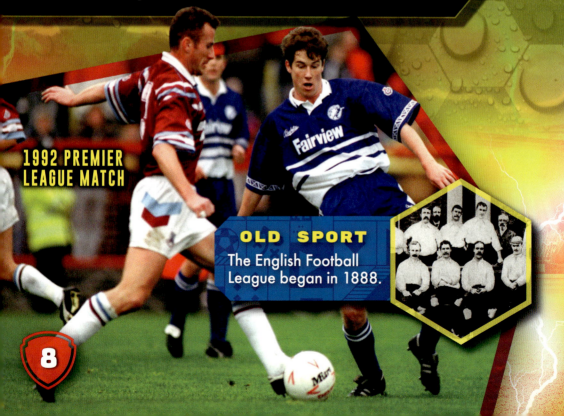

1992 PREMIER LEAGUE MATCH

OLD SPORT
The English Football League began in 1888.

FOUNDING TEAMS

- ARSENAL
- ASTON VILLA
- BLACKBURN ROVERS
- CHELSEA
- COVENTRY CITY
- CRYSTAL PALACE
- EVERTON
- IPSWICH TOWN
- LEEDS UNITED
- LIVERPOOL
- MANCHESTER CITY
- MANCHESTER UNITED
- MIDDLESBROUGH
- NORWICH CITY
- NOTTINGHAM FOREST
- OLDHAM ATHLETIC
- QUEENS PARK RANGERS
- SHEFFIELD UNITED
- SHEFFIELD WEDNESDAY
- SOUTHAMPTON
- TOTTENHAM HOTSPUR
- WIMBLEDON

9

There were 22 teams in the first Premier League season. The number of teams was lowered to 20 in 1995. This was done to increase the quality of other soccer leagues in England.

In 2019, the Premier League began using **Video Assistant Referee**. This helps referees make the right calls.

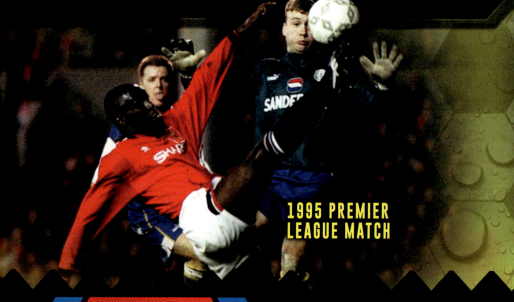

1995 PREMIER LEAGUE MATCH

TIMELINE

1888
The English Football League begins

1991
Teams agree to form the Premier League

1992
The Premier League becomes the top level of soccer in England

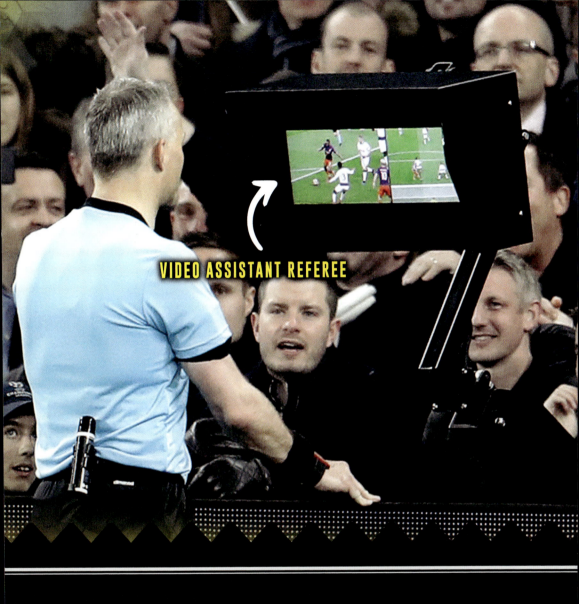

VIDEO ASSISTANT REFEREE

1995
The number of teams in the league drops from 22 to 20

2019
Video Assistant Referee is first used in league games

THE PREMIER LEAGUE TODAY

The Premier League season usually begins in August. It ends in May. There are 38 match days each season. Each team plays all the other teams twice per season. One of these matches is played at home. The other is away.

Teams earn three points for winning a match. One point is earned for a draw. Zero points are earned for a loss.

The teams that play in the Premier League change each season. The three teams with the fewest points at the end of the season are **relegated**. They move to the **Championship League**.

The top two teams from the Championship League are **promoted** to the Premier League. The next four teams in the Championship League play in a **playoff**. The winner is promoted.

2023 CHAMPIONSHIP LEAGUE PLAYOFF MATCH

THE REGULARS
There are six Premier League teams that have never been relegated.

RELEGATION AND PROMOTION

1. RELEGATION
The bottom three Premier League teams are relegated.

2. PROMOTION
The top two Championship League teams are promoted.

3. PLAYOFFS
The teams that placed third through sixth in the Championship League play in a playoff series, with the winner being promoted.

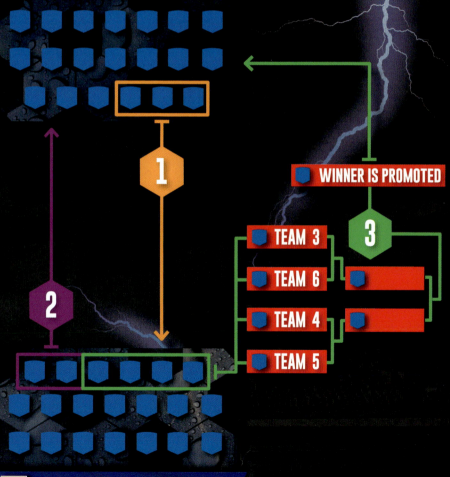

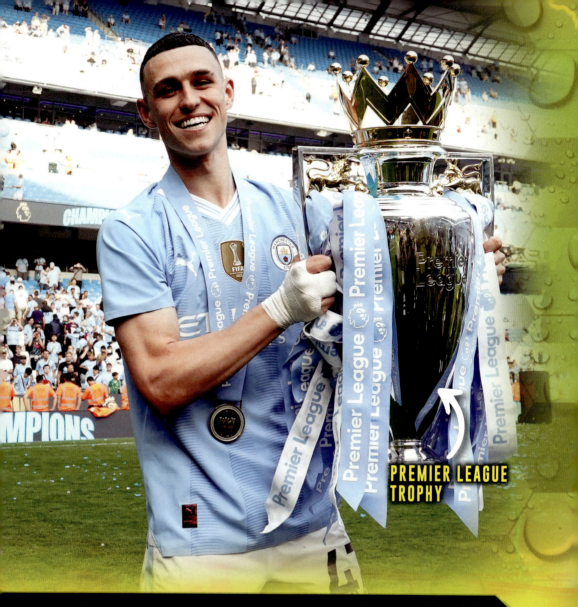

PREMIER LEAGUE TROPHY

The team with the most points at the end of the season wins the Premier League. Sometimes two teams have the same number of points. The tiebreaker is **goal difference**.

There are awards each season for the player and **manager** of the season. There are also awards for the best young player and for the most powerful goal.

Premier League teams also play in the **FA Cup**. They play against teams from other English soccer leagues. The final unbeaten team wins the Cup!

The top four Premier League teams also earn a spot in the **Champions League**. There are many ways fans can watch their favorite Premier League team play!

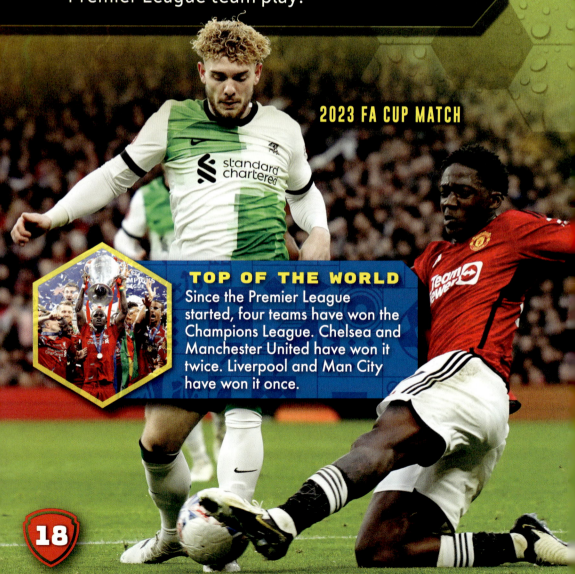

2023 FA CUP MATCH

TOP OF THE WORLD
Since the Premier League started, four teams have won the Champions League. Chelsea and Manchester United have won it twice. Liverpool and Man City have won it once.

TOP PLAYERS

ALAN SHEARER

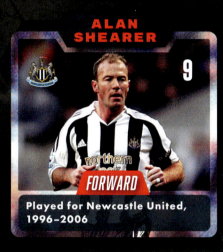

9
FORWARD

Played for Newcastle United, 1996–2006

THIERRY HENRY

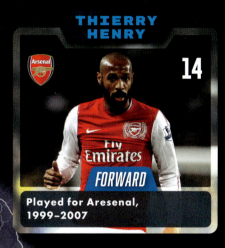

14
FORWARD

Played for Aresenal, 1999–2007

CRISTIANO RONALDO

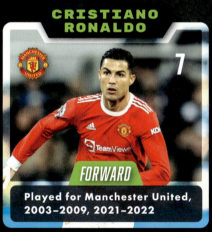

7
FORWARD

Played for Manchester United, 2003–2009, 2021–2022

WAYNE ROONEY

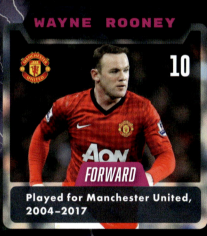

10
FORWARD

Played for Manchester United, 2004–2017

ERLING HAALAND

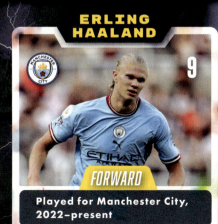

9
FORWARD

Played for Manchester City, 2022–present

19

FAST FACTS

| NUMBER OF TEAMS | 20 |
| YEAR STARTED | 1992 |

LARGEST STADIUM

OLD TRAFFORD
MANCHESTER UNITED

Capacity: more than 74,000 people
Location: Manchester, England

CLUB RECORDS
(AS OF 2023)

CLUBS WITH MOST APPEARANCES
ARSENAL, CHELSEA, EVERTON, LIVERPOOL, MANCHESTER UNITED, TOTTENHAM HOTSPUR

32 seasons

CLUB WITH MOST CHAMPIONSHIPS
MANCHESTER UNITED

13

FIRST CHAMPION
MANCHESTER UNITED

CLUBS THAT HAVE PARTICIPATED IN THE LEAGUE

51

INDIVIDUAL RECORDS
(AS OF 2023)

Most career league goals
Alan Shearer: 260 goals

Most goals scored in a single season
Erling Haaland: 36 goals

Fastest goal scored
Shane Long: 7.69 seconds

Person with most league appearances
Gareth Barry: 653 appearances

GLOSSARY

Champions League—a European soccer tournament where the top teams of the top European leagues play each other to decide the best team in Europe

Championship League—the second level of professional soccer in England

division—level

extra time—time added to the end of soccer matches to make up for stoppages

FA Cup—the championship tournament for professional soccer in England and Wales

goal difference—the number of goals scored by a team minus the number of goals allowed by the team

goals—scores in soccer; players score goals by sending the ball into the other team's net.

manager—a person who directs a soccer team

playoff—a series of matches played after the regular season is over; playoff matches determine which team plays in the Premier League the next season.

professional—related to a player or team that makes money playing a sport

promoted—moved up to a higher league

relegated—moved down to a lower league

Video Assistant Referee—a referee who watches video of the match to help referees on the field make decisions; Video Assistant Referee is often called VAR.

TO LEARN MORE

AT THE LIBRARY

Gish, Ashley. *La Liga*. Minneapolis, Minn.: Bellwether Media, 2025.

Goldblatt, David. *The Soccer Book: The Teams, The Rules, The Leagues, The Tactics*. New York, N.Y.: DK Publishing, 2021.

Golkar, Golriz. *Cristiano Ronaldo*. Minneapolis, Minn.: Bellwether Media, 2024.

ON THE WEB

Factsurfer.com gives you a safe, fun way to find more information.

1. Go to www.factsurfer.com

2. Enter "Premier League" into the search box and click 🔍.

3. Select your book cover to see a list of related content.

INDEX

awards, 17
Champions League, 18
Championship
  League, 14
division, 8
England, 6, 8, 10, 18
English Football
  League, 8
extra time, 4
FA Cup, 18
fans, 7, 18
fast facts, 20–21
founding teams, 9
goal difference, 16
goals, 4, 16, 17
history, 4, 8, 9, 10, 18
manager, 17
match, 8, 10, 12, 13, 18

players, 7, 8, 17, 19
playoff, 14
points, 13, 14, 16
promoted, 14
referees, 10
relegated, 14
relegation and
  promotion, 15
season, 4, 6, 8, 10, 12,
  14, 16
teams, 4, 6, 7, 8, 9, 10,
  12, 13, 14, 16, 18
timeline, 10–11
top players, 19
Video Assistant Referee,
  10, 11
Wales, 6, 8

The images in this book are reproduced through the courtesy of: Sportimage Ltd/ Alamy, cover, pp. 3, 14 (2023 Championship League playoff match); Martin Rickett/ AP Images, pp. 4, 4-5; PA Images/ Alamy, pp. 6, 7, 8 (1992 Premier League Match, Old Sport), 10 (1995 Premier League match, 1888, 1991), 11 (1995), 19 (Alan Shearer, Thierry Henry, Wayne Rooney), 21 (Shane Long); Premier League/ Wiki Commons, pp. 9 (logos), 10 (1991), 20 (Premier League logo); Adam Davy/ AP Images, p. 11 (Video Assistant Referee); Mark Kerton/ AP Images, p. 11 (2019); Andrew Yates/ AP Images, p. 12; Paul Terry/ AP Images, pp. 13, 16; MatchDay Images Limited/ DW/ Alamy, pp. 14 (The Regulars), 20; Arron Gent/ News Images/ AP Images, p. 17; Andrew Yates/ AP Images, p. 18 (2023 FA Cup match); SOPA Images Limited/ Alamy, p. 18 (Top of the World); News Images Ltd/ Alamy, p. 19 (Cristiano Ronaldo); Allstar Picture Library Ltd/ Alamy, pp. 19 (Erling Haaland), 21 (Alan Shearer, Gareth Barry); Wirestock Creators, p. 20 (Old Trafford); Andrew Orchard sports photography/ Alamy, p. 21 (Erling Haaland); Cosmin Iftode, p. 23.